Joint Ventures Made Easy

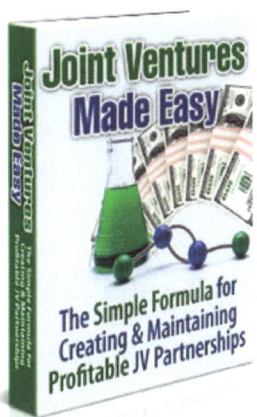

The Simple Formula for Creating and Maintaining Profitable JV Partnerships

By JayKay Bak

Legal Notice:- This digital eBook is for informational purposes only. While every attempt has been made to verify the information provided in this report, neither the author, publisher nor the marketer assume any responsibility for errors or omissions. Any slights of people or organizations are unintentional and the development of this eBook is bona fide. The producer and marketer have no intention whatsoever to convey any idea affecting the reputation of any person or business enterprise. The trademarks, screen-shots, website links, products and services mentioned in this eBook are copyrighted by their respective owners. This eBook has been distributed with the understanding that we are not engaged in rendering technical, legal, medical, accounting or other professional advice. We do not give any kind of guarantee about the accuracy of information provided. In no event will the author and/or marketer be liable for any direct, indirect, incidental, consequential or other loss or damage arising out of the use of the information in this document by any person, regardless of whether or not informed of the possibility of damages in advance. Thank you for your attention to this message.

Table of Contents

Introduction - Keys To A Successful Joint Venture 3
Chapter 1 – What Is A Joint Venture? 3
Chapter 2 – Who Should Consider A Joint Venture? 5
Chapter 3 – Where To Meet Joint Venture Partners 7
Chapter 4 – What To Look For In Joint Venture Partners 10
Chapter 5 – Ways To Hold Your Joint Venture 12
Chapter 6 – Using A Joint Venture Broker 14
Chapter 7 – Meeting Joint Venture Partners Online 15
Chapter 8 – Starting A Joint Venture With A Foreign Entity 17
Chapter 9 – Marketing Your Joint Venture 19
Chapter 10 – Starting Your Joint Venture 21
Chapter 11 – 10 Reasons To Start A Joint Venture 23
Chapter 12 – What Can Go Wrong In A Joint Venture 24
Chapter 13 – Keeping Your Joint Venture Going Strong 25

Introduction - Keys To A Successful Joint Venture

A joint venture can afford your business to grow in ways that you never would have dreamed of 20 years ago. Today, thanks to the internet, more people are forming joint ventures with one another and becoming successful because of them. There are joint ventures that are formed with people from all over the globe that are booming. Not only are people making money, but they are getting to experience different cultures and marketing plans. Those who are involved in such ventures are finding that they are not only making a profit, but growing as people at the same time.

The world is no longer large. The internet has allowed us to get connected to people we otherwise might not have met. One way that people are connecting is through business. Savvy business owners and investors are discovering joint ventures and how they can help them expand their current businesses as well as teach them business tips that they can use in the future.

In order to create, maintain and grow the best joint ventures, you have to understand everything about a joint venture such as what it is, what makes it such a viable option in today's business climate and how it can help your business. This book will explain to you everything that you need to know about joint ventures including how you can form the best type of joint venture for you.

Chapter 1 - What Is A Joint Venture?

You have probably heard about joint ventures as they have become more common in the past few years, especially with regard to investing. But what is a joint venture? If you are like most people, you may have assumed that it was a type of entity.

A joint venture is not a separate entity. It is comprised of either individuals or businesses for the purpose of a single project. It is a partnership between two or more individuals, corporations, LLCs or other entities for a single purpose. This can range from investing in a foreclosure to a shopping mall. A joint venture is a type of partnership that has a limited purpose.

In order to set up a joint venture, you must meet with the other principals of the venture and draw up a legal contract. The contract will specify the purpose of the joint venture, the duties of all of the principals and how the property or assets of the joint venture can be owned. The joint venture can be a corporation, a partnership or an LLC. What makes a joint venture different is that it is not an entity in itself, rather, it is formed for a specific purpose, which makes it the joint venture.

One common use for a joint venture is for home investments. Many people today are looking to invest in real estate. The fact that the real estate market is at the bottom has made many investors stand up and take notice as this is an excellent opportunity to buy. However, not everyone has money in which to invest in property. This is where the joint venture comes in.

A joint venture can pair one person up with money who does not have the time nor the inclination to look for foreclosures and short sales, with another individual who has all the time and expertise in the world but not any money. The two parties can agree on a joint venture.

Unlike a partnership, a joint venture puts a limit on the liabilities of both of the parties and a limit on their involvement with one another. Whereas a partnership seems to link individuals together for many projects and is an ongoing entity, a joint venture is specifically formed for the sole purpose of one specific project.

If you decided to get into a joint venture with another individual to purchase a house, you could each own the property as individuals or by any entity under which you are operating. A corporation can team up with an LLC. An individual can team up with a corporation.

The joint venture papers are a contract usually drawn up in the office of an attorney who is knowledgeable in corporate law. The joint venture contract specifies the duties of each principal in the venture as well as how any assets will be split. The project is specified in the agreement, making the joint venture a unique type of entity all of its own.

Each principal in a joint venture should be well aware of their duties within the venture as well as how much they can expect to make for the joint venture. Because a joint venture targets a specific project, it is usually of a short duration. If, in the above example, two people decided to get together to invest in a foreclosure property, the joint venture would end when the property was sold and the profit was made. The money from the profit would be transferred into the joint venture and then distributed, in accordance with the agreement, to the parties involved.

If the parties decided that they enjoyed the business relationship and all are happy with the outcome, they can then embark in another joint venture. They will have to draw up another agreement for another property and then go through the entire process again. As time wears on and the parties decide that they like working with one another, they can form a limited partnership, an LLC or a corporation that is not a joint venture, but one where they have several different ongoing projects.

A joint venture works for individuals or entities that are interested in forming a business partnership with others over a specific project. It does not work for those who want to form a lasting partnership with another individual, although it can be a good way to see if you like working with another company or individual. As a matter of fact, some successful businesses have started as joint ventures. Because liability is limited to one specific project, this gives everyone a chance to get to know the other parties in the venture and decide whether or not they want this to be a lasting relationship.

Building a joint venture into a lasting business relationship is well worth the time and effort as you can certainly afford to do more with a joint venture than you can in your own business. If you are looking to diversify your business as well as expand, a joint venture can give you this opportunity without costing you a lot of investment capital.

Chapter 2 - Who Should Consider A Joint Venture?

Any business that is seeking to expand can consider a joint venture, especially if they are looking to grow in uncharted territory. A joint venture can give individuals and businesses an opportunity to take their business to a different level.

Some uses for a joint venture would be the following:

- Investing in building a shopping center
- Investing in foreclosed houses or short sales
- Any short term investment
- Expanding a business to include a new line of products or services

All of the above could benefit from developing a joint venture. Here's how:

Investing in a shopping center

It doesn't have to be a shopping center, it can be any large investment. This can encompass any large investment that requires a lot of capital. If you take a look around at strip malls and shopping centers, you will see that most of them are owned by businesses that are involved in a joint venture.

When it comes to a large investment with some amount of risk but the potential for a high return, most people will not want to take all of their capital to invest in property. Because of the risk entailed, most investors would rather just invest a portion of their capital in such a venture. But where do you get the rest of the money?

This is where the joint venture comes in to play. Instead of one business or individual investing a good portion of his capital in this potential money making investment, several entities form a joint venture for this type of investment. Some may just contribute capital while others may contribute knowledge. The terms of the joint venture as well as who gets what type of profit are spelled out before the project begins.

Take a look around and you will see that many strip malls and shopping centers are held by joint ventures. They are usually a mixture of investors and developers. Developers will use investors such as professional people who are looking for a high yield on their investment, to finance projects like strip malls and shopping centers as they will end up paying less money in interest to the bank.

One way for you to make a joint venture work for you is if you have either capital or knowledge of some sort. You can then team up with others who can either provide expertise or money in order to make a project work for all involved. By investing in a large investment such as a shopping center as part of a joint venture, you cut down your financial risk.

Investing in foreclosures or short sales

You have probably heard about people who are investing in the real estate market using "no money down." or investment gurus who promise you ways to make money in the real estate market without using your own cash. This is how they are doing this. Joint ventures are the way that a lot of investors are using to make money in the real estate market, even in this down market, without investing any of their own capital. They find someone who has money to invest but does not know the real estate market and present their plan to them. The person, people or business with the money will want to see a business plan and a proven track record of how you can make money for your investors. You will then show them how you have invested in foreclosures in the past, how much you need to make the deal on the foreclosure and how much you can expect to sell the house for.

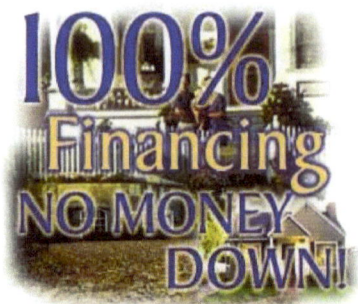

For example, if you have a foreclosure that you think you can get for $150,000 but will be worth $400,000 after you make some cosmetic repairs, you can give your investors all of this information. Their investment will be $150,000 of which they stand to make a profit of $200,000 after the house is sold. You can take $50,000 for your efforts and not have to put out a dime. You will have to show the investors how much work needs to be done, comparable prices in the neighborhood (with regard to the estimated sales price and revenue) and your track record. The reason the investors will want to go into a joint venture with you in such a case would be because;

- They know nothing about buying a foreclosure but think this is a good deal
- They do not have the time nor inclination to make repairs in the house
- They want a high return in a short amount of time

When you think about it, for an investor to make more than double their investment in less than a year is a good opportunity. But in order to convince others to join in a joint venture with you, you are going to have to prove that you know the real estate business inside and out.

Any short term investment

A joint venture will work with any type of short term investment. Because a joint venture is concentrated on a particular project, it is the ideal way to invest short term. Whether you are looking to invest in real estate or a short business venture, a joint venture is a good opportunity.

You will not usually see a joint venture in the restaurant business or other long term business. The reason for this is because these businesses are expected to stay in operation for a long period of time. A joint venture is usually more of a type of investment than anything else. If the business opportunity is long term, then the parties will usually enter into a long term agreement, such as a corporation or limited partnership.

Expanding a business to include a new line of products or services

By using a joint venture as a way to expand your business to include a new line of products or services, you can then see if your business will profit with this new business line. A joint venture is a good way to test the waters when it comes to expanding a business, especially if you are getting into something new.

For example, if you have a business that sells sunglasses and you are approached by someone who wants you to sell designer purses, you may consider going in to a joint venture with someone who is selling designer purses. The joint venture can give both of you a chance to see how your business fares by selling more than one product. You would then set up a joint venture of a sunglasses and purses business and see how it does. Neither party has put out any extra capital as you both merely took from your own inventory for the new joint venture. You may split advertising costs and the cost for developing a website. You can give your new business a name and even incorporate it, but you are not giving up your standing business of selling sunglasses.

If the new business is a success, you may consider a merger with the other party. If you enjoy working with the other principal in the joint venture, you may consider a partnership or forming a corporation with them so that you can continue the sunglasses and designer purse business on a long term basis and take advantage of tax breaks allotted to small businesses.

A joint venture is an ideal way to invest in a short term vehicle or to test the waters with a new partner or entity with whom you are thinking of doing business. It does not work in the long term scale as it does not afford the tax benefits of a corporation, LLC or even a limited partnership. It is meant only as an investment for a specific short term purpose.

If you have been thinking about investing in property or a business but are hesitant about using all of your capital in which to do so, you should consider a joint venture. Although you will not be able to reap all of the profits from the joint venture, you will not incur all of the risk, either. A joint venture spreads the risk around, as well as the proceeds, to everyone involved.

Chapter 3 - Where To Meet Joint Venture Partners

You may be thinking that you would like to go into business, or maybe invest in the real estate market, but do not want to go it alone. You need a partner who has something that you do not have - or is just willing to help out and share the risk. Where to do you find those who are interested in a joint venture?

Ideally, you would form a joint venture with people who you know and trust - like family members. It does not always work out this way, however. In many cases, you will form a joint venture with someone who you have never met before but who is interested in the same project.

You can meet joint venture partners in a variety of different ways. Here are some, to name a few:

- Investment clubs
- Word of mouth
- Online joint venture sites
- Joint venture brokers

All of the above have advantages when it comes to forming a joint venture and all are relatively easy to find. Here is how you can use the above ways to meet a joint venture partner:

Investment clubs

Investment clubs are created by a variety of people who all have something in common - they want to invest their money so that they can make money,. Money sitting in a bank does not even earn 3 percent interest - people today, more than ever, realize that there has to be a better way.

Investment clubs have been around for a long time. People often formed investment clubs to speculate on stocks. This is where the idea of mutual funds comes from. There are many avenues open for someone who wants to invest in stock with others. But what about those who want a different type of investment that can promise them even more money when it comes to a return?

Investment clubs allow people who want to use their money to make money to meet with one another and decide what is the type of investment for them. By joining an investment club, you can be privy to the types of investments that different people seek. If you have an idea that can benefit the investment club, you can offer individuals an opportunity to get in on the ground floor of your joint venture. Again, when presenting any idea to people where you are going to ask them to part with their money, you had better know your investment inside and out. You do not want to have any unanswered questions or you are unlikely to gain anyone's confidence and thus get investors in your joint venture.

Word of Mouth

This is a good way to meet others who are like minded and will share your interest in a joint venture. Whenever you are serious about any type of business, you should have cards printed up with your name, name of your business and contact information. There are places online that will print up business cards for you for free. Whenever you go anywhere, you should be sure to talk about your business to just about anyone who will listen. Think of a way to work it into the conversation. Your business should be an extension of you so it should come naturally for you to talk about it. You would be surprised at the people you will meet who may share your passion and be interested in investing or learning more about your joint venture. Bring business cards with you whenever you go out so that you do not miss an opportunity to form a relationship with a prospective joint venture partner.

While meeting people by word of mouth is a good way to be able to assess them right away and get to know them quickly, it also takes time. You should not limit yourself to only meeting people through word of mouth or chance encounters. Exhaust all avenues when looking for fellow principals in joint ventures.

Online joint venture sites

Thanks to the internet, it is easier than ever for people to find others with whom they share interests, even those who want to start businesses or investment opportunities. Naturally, when meeting strangers online, you have to protect your interests, but you will have to do that no matter who you go into business with. As a matter of fact, some of the most volatile business relationships are between family members. The reason for this is that while people automatically assume that they have to protect their business interests against strangers, they often let down their guard with family members. This can cause quite a bit of problems if an inlaw or third party gets into the mix.

Online joint venture sites are a great way for people who are looking to start a joint venture can meet others who also have something to bring to the table. Naturally, you will want to go slowly with your new potential partners and make sure that everything is done in a legal way. Because the internet gives us access to people we would not otherwise meet, there is a lot of potential when it comes to finding joint venture principals and either starting a business, expanding a business or making an investment.

Joint Venture Brokers

Joint venture brokers are individuals who will find like minded individuals and hook them up with one another, usually for a percentage of the profit in the joint venture or a fee. Some online joint venture websites effectively act as joint venture brokers in that they charge a fee to join the site.

It can be well worth your money to pay someone to find a good investment partner for you, especially if they are getting a percentage of any slated profits. This is because the broker then has a stake in the investment as well. If you are looking for an individual or company with which to form a joint venture and need to find someone in a hurry, using a joint venture broker is the best option as they can usually move a lot quicker and hook you up with potential business partners in a hurry.

You can find joint venture partners in a variety of different venues. Once you understand the concept of a joint venture and how you can make such a vehicle work for you, you will be more in tune with others, their needs and opportunities that present themselves to you on a daily basis that you do not even notice.

When looking for joint venture partners, make sure that you try all of the above methods. The more people who you get to know who are interested in investing, the better your chances of finding the perfect principals for your joint venture.

Looking for joint venture principals is much like looking for a mate. You should leave no stone unturned and realize that the more people you get to know, the better your chances of finding Mr. or Mrs. Right. In the case of a joint venture, you may find more than one person who will fit the bill for what you have in mind for your joint venture and, unlike a personal relationship, the more the merrier. The more people who are willing to invest in your project, the better for everyone as the less risk that is involved.

Chapter 4 - What To Look For In Joint Venture Partners

When you are looking for joint venture partners, there are a variety of different qualities that you should look for in an individual. Again, looking for business partners is much like looking for a person with whom you want to have a personal relationship. As a matter of fact, it is very similar as you will be forming a relationship of sorts with the individuals or businesses that you find. About the only thing that will be left out is that you will not have to have physical chemistry with the people with whom you form a joint venture. Some of the qualities that you will look for include:

- Integrity
- Qualifications
- Experience
- Capital

All of these are important when you are looking for a business partner. Although a joint venture is not a permanent arrangement, it is good to look at it as if you are going to be in business for a long time to come. Look for these attributes in either a business or individual whenever you mingle your name with theirs:

Integrity

Not only do you want those in your joint venture to have integrity and be able to count on them to do the right thing by you, but also by other people. Remember that people tend to judge you by the company that you keep. If you are involved in a joint venture with another individual or company that is not above the board with everything, your good name might be dragged down with theirs.

Make sure that you trust your partners as much as you can when entering into a joint venture. You do not want to always feel that you have to be looking over your shoulder whenever you are in any type of relationship with anyone, even a business relationship. That being said , while you will want to establish trust with those in your joint venture, you should not abandon legalities. Make sure that everything is spelled out in a legally binding contract with regard to the joint venture.

Remember that whatever your partners in the joint venture do will reflect unto you. The old saying "if you lay down with dogs, you'll get up with fleas" rings true, even when you are talking about a short term proposition like a joint venture.

Qualifications

Naturally, if you are planning on investing in a joint venture with another individual, they should have qualifications for the investment. They should be bringing something to the table other than their appearance. If someone is more qualified than you with regard to the joint venture and project, they will probably want more of a share of the profits. This may work out well for you as you can use them to mentor you with regard to the business. Even if you are not getting the lion's share of the profits, you will still be making money and also learning a thing or two from a qualified individual. If you do not have a lot of experience, you should look for someone with more qualifications than you to start your joint venture.

Experience

If you are seeking to put your money into a joint venture to get a high return, you naturally will want to look for a joint venture partner who has vast experience in the type of venture that you are entering into. If you have vast experience in a field, such as foreclosures or real estate investing, you may look for someone with capital to invest, although they should be able to understand what it is you are doing. Two businesses may join in a joint venture, both with moderate experience - seeking to gain further knowledge. In such a case, the business owners can learn from one another.

Always look at any joint venture as a chance to further not only your capital and business, but also your knowledge.

Capital

How much money does the other party or parties have? How much are they willing to put up towards the joint venture. While not everyone has to put up an equal share with regard to the joint venture, the amount that they take back with regard to proceeds should reflect the percentage of their investment.

Naturally, someone who is putting up more than 50 percent of the share in the joint venture, with regard to capital, should not be expected to take just 50 percent of the profits. Most people will want the same percentage in returns as they put forth in their investment.

It is a good idea to go into a joint venture with someone who has some money and has something to lose. If you go into a venture with another individual who is not putting forth any of his own money towards the project, he does not have much on the line. The exception to this would be if you are involved in a large joint venture with other investors with someone who is an expert in a certain field. The example that was given earlier in this book regarding a person who knows the ins and outs of real estate investing and is investing in short sales and foreclosures for a group of investors would be an exception. In such a case, a party in the joint venture brings forth their own special expertise to the project.

All of the principals in a joint venture should have an incentive to make sure the project works. As long as everyone is properly motivated, the project has a better chance of working than if some people do not care if it sinks or swims. Choose your partners in a joint venture wisely.

Chapter 5 - Ways To Hold Your Joint Venture

As we said earlier, a joint venture is not an entity, but the reason for the entity. A joint venture can be individuals, corporations, LLCs or even limited partnerships. There are tax advantages to all of these types of holdings. How you should hold your joint venture depends upon the size of the project and how long you plan to be involved in the project.

Corporation

A corporation is a separate entity. It can open a bank account, pay taxes and go bankrupt. Because a corporation is its own entity, it is the safest way to start a business. By funneling everything into the corporation, you limit the liability of the other parties.

Two corporations or other types of business can form another corporation. A corporation will need people, however, to be officers of the entity. You also need a registered agent. The registered agent is usually the attorney who fills out the articles of incorporation and will keep up with the annual reports.

There are two types of corporations - a C corporation and an S corporation. You will most likely charter your joint venture under an S charter in that you will not be selling stocks. An S corporation, or a Sub S, as it is often called, is limited to the number of shares of stock it can issue. An S corporation can only issue 100 shares of stock.

The stockholders are the real power in the corporation. The stockholders do not have to be the same people who are officers of the corporation. They can be businesses or individuals. Their ownership of the corporation is not made public - the officers and registered agent are public information.

A corporation has tax benefits that are not afforded to individuals. That and the fact that by putting everything into a corporation puts a limit on the liability of those involved in the corporation makes it an attractive entity to consider when you are considering how to hold a joint venture.

LLC

An LLC is a limited liability company. Like a corporation, you have to file the LLC with the state. The filing fees are usually higher for an LLC, but this type of company offers the same protection as a corporation in that it is its own entity, but without the cumbersome paperwork that is involved in maintaining a corporation. A corporation is obligated to have regular meetings and keep minutes of the meetings. An LLC does not have the same obligation and is an easier type of entity to maintain. Because it gets the same type of tax breaks and offers the principals the same protection as a corporation, this type of entity is often preferred over a Sub S corporation. You cannot sell stock in an LLC.

Limited Partnership

Some people confuse a limited partnership with a joint venture. A limited partnership is an entity between two or more individuals for no specified period of time or for a particular project. A joint venture is similar to a limited partnership in that it is a legally binding agreement between two or more individuals, but whereas the limited partnership is not limited to a specific project or endeavor, the joint venture is. And the joint venture can be comprised of many different types of entities.

Sole proprietorship

You can set up shop and open up your own business as a sole proprietor without having to file any paperwork with the state or even talk to an attorney. The free enterprise system allows anyone to just start a business as a sole proprietor. You will have to claim income taxes on this business, but can do so on your individual income tax statement. You will have to file a Schedule C for a sole proprietor business. You can enter into a joint venture as a sole proprietor, but be aware that you are offered no personal protection. If the joint venture files bankruptcy, you may be also finding yourself in bankruptcy court. The same goes if the joint venture is sued. If you own your business as a sole proprietor, you will want to make sure that the joint venture is held in a protective entity such as a corporation or LLC.

If the joint venture is held as a sole proprietorship, then any liability for the joint venture will fall upon the entities or individuals that make up the joint venture.

Individual ownership

If you are not worried about liability and are in a small joint venture with another individual, you can each take ownership of anything in the joint venture as individuals. If, for example, you form a joint venture with someone to purchase a foreclosed house, you can each take ownership of the property as tenants in common. Any assets that the joint venture owns should be held by each of you as tenants in common.

Prior to joint ventures, corporations, limited partnerships and LLCs, it was not unusual for people in business with one another to manage their business by making sure that all assets and liabilities were held as tenants in common. Tenants in common means that both parties are owners of the asset. Unlike joint tenants, when property or other assets is held as tenants in common, and one of the tenants dies, the heirs of the deceased party will be entitled to their share of the assets. With joint tenancy, the other partner would be able to claim the assets as their own.

Before our society became so litigious, it was not unusual for parties to strike out a verbal agreement and hold assets and property as tenants in common. Today, however, you are better off to gain the protection of a protective entity such as a corporation, limited partnership or LLC when you are entering the business world.

Chapter 6 - Using A Joint Venture Broker

There are many ways that you can find a joint venture broker to help you find the perfect person to help form your joint venture. Thanks to the internet, it is now easier than ever to meet different people whom you would not otherwise meet. This is especially true when it comes to meeting fellow investors or business owners.

You can find a joint venture broker either online or offine. The purpose of the joint venture broker is to bring together people who are looking for an investment of some sort, so that they can have a joint venture. When looking for a joint venture broker, you should consider the following:

- How much success has the broker had?
- What type of fee will I be expected to pay?
- How does the broker screen the prospects?

Naturally, you will want to consider all three of these questions very carefully when you are looking for a joint venture broker.

How much success has the broker had?

Experience counts when you are looking for anyone who is going to be responsible for setting you up in business with someone else. You will want to find a joint venture broker who has experience and who has been working with joint venture investors for some time.

Find a joint venture broker who has been in business for a while. Look for experience first and then worry about price. When you are first starting out in setting up a joint venture, you will want to get a good broker who you can trust to help you find the perfect joint venture partner.

If the joint venture broker has had quite a bit of success in finding prospect for joint ventures, they should give you some names of references with regard to their client base. You should check out the references and see how they liked working with the broker and whether they found their endeavor profitable.

What type of fee will I be expected to pay?

In most cases, you will be expected to pay a small fee to the broker for their service. They may charge a commission off of the project or a flat fee up front. If you find a joint venture broker online, you will most likely pay a fee to belong to their site. There are many different sites online that allow you to find others who want to start a joint venture. Most of these sites will expect you to pay a fee to join the site. This fee will alleviate any fee that you will have to pay when you meet someone with whom you want to start a joint venture.

Many people who are just starting out and want to start a joint venture will look at online joint venture clubs. Not only are these clubs effective at helping you find the perfect joint venture partner, but you can pay a small fee and have access to the different marketing tools and forums suggested by members of the club. If you are just starting out in business and looking for someone with whom you can start a joint venture, you are better off to join an online site where you can not only meet other people but also take advantage of marketing tools.

How does the broker screen the prospects?

You will want to find a broker or a website that offers a bit of screening for your joint venture prospects. This is why it is a good idea to go to a paid site. A paid site will screen out a lot of people who might not be serious about starting a joint venture. At least if you are paying for membership on a site, you have a good chance of finding that most, if not all of the people who are the site are also looking for the same thing as you.

Regardless of how well your joint venture broker screens potential joint venture partners, never rely solely on a third party to do this vital job for you. Use discretion when you meet anyone for the first time, especially when you meet someone with whom you are planning on doing business. Whether or not the broker screens the prospects, you still should be prudent when you are dealing with potential business partners.

Chapter 7 - Meeting Joint Venture Partners Online

There are various ways to meet joint venture partners, especially online. The internet gives us access to people whom we never would have met 20 years ago. This can be good and bad.

Find a site online where you can meet a joint venture partner and, once you feel comfortable, join the site. Do not look for someone right away. Participate in the forums and try to get to know people on the site.

Beware of anyone who comes on too strong or offers you a deal that is too good to be true. Just like any other type of social interaction forum, a joint venture site is filled with predators. If someone offers you a deal that is designed to make you part with your money, forget it.

Here are some things to look out for when you are seeking joint venture partners online:

- People who come on too strong
- People who try to find out personal information about you or your business
- People who want you to do all of the work
- People who offer you a lot of money for not doing anything

People who come on too strong usually have something up their sleeve that involves you spending your money while they collect it. Someone who approaches you and will not let you alone, or who calls you on the phone constantly is probably trying to sell their own product instead of offering you a legitimate chance of getting into a joint venture. Beware of such types and just tell them that you are not interested. If they persist to harass you, contact the site administrator.

You should not give out any personal information about yourself or your business just because someone asks. Remember that phishing goes on all over the internet and that a business website is an ideal place for an unscrupulous character to try to find out information about you that they can use for their own gain. Never give out personal or business information to anyone who you just met online, regardless of the site. The site that you join should also be one that is willing to protect your privacy.

Just like everywhere else, you may find someone who wants to be in a joint venture but does not have any money nor are they any sort of industry expert. In other words, they want to ride along on your gravy train. They may have a good gift of gab, but they are a bad prospect when it comes to finding a joint venture partner. Beware of the charmers who really have nothing substantial to offer you and just look good on the surface.

You should also be careful of anyone who offers you a lot of money to do nothing. The old "Nigerian check scam" costs individuals billions of dollars a year. Yes, that's right, billions. As long as there are greedy people around who want to get something for nothing, the Nigerian check scam will continue to flourish.

The way that this scam works, in case you don't know, is that someone offers you a substantial amount of money to help them out. They are usually trapped in some foreign country and someone has given them money. They have a check but cannot cash it. They ask to send the check to you and ask you to cash it, keep a portion of the check for yourself and then send them the remainder. The check is a phony. The bank then comes back to you for trying to pass a phony money order or check. The money that you send to the person (usually in Nigeria, but it could be anywhere) is long gone. So is the person. You are out a substantial amount of money.

If someone offers you money for doing nothing, chances are that it is one of the many variations of the Nigerian check scam or they are doing something illegal. Stay away from such individuals.

When you start out looking for a joint venture partner, look for someone who has interests similar to your own and who will add to your business. You should always look for someone who is a step ahead of you in the business world so that you can learn from them. Remember to look at each joint venture as a way to learn more about your business as well as a way to make money.

Chapter 8 - Starting A Joint Venture With A Foreign Entity

One of the primary reasons why people start a joint venture is to have a business venture that is legally binding with a foreign entity. In the United States, a foreign person or entity cannot incorporate a business. Many people who wish to start businesses with those in other countries do so by starting up a joint venture. This can join two businesses from two different countries and allow them to form one business.

When you start a joint venture with a foreign entity, you cannot incorporate the joint venture. You can, if it is okay with the other party, form an LLC, but in most cases, the other party will not want to be bound to laws in a state where they do not live.

When you start a joint venture with a foreign entity, you will most likely take assets as individuals or as sole proprietors. You will most likely not form a separate entity for the joint venture. The two of you will most likely come to some agreement between you and then work from there. The agreement can be in writing or it can be a verbal agreement.

There are sites online that will act as escrow agents when you are starting a joint venture with a foreign entity. You may each be able to deposit a certain amount of money in to the escrow for the venture. You can have a neutral party oversee the escrow account.

It can be difficult to get started in a joint venture with a foreign entity. There are pros and cons to this sort of arrangement. On the positive side, being in a joint venture with a foreign entity can do the following for your business:

- Allow you to sell your product or services to other areas of the world
- Allow you to receive products or services from other areas of the world
- Allow you to expand your business into other areas of the world
- Give you valuable insight as to marketing strategies in other parts of the world

If you are going to expand in your business, you should look to move throughout the world. With the advent of the internet, the world is not such a big, scary place any longer. People from other countries are constantly doing business with one another. The internet has made it possible for businesses to grow and prosper in places they never thought possible.

Perhaps you have a small store in the United States. You want to offer your customers something different that they cannot anywhere else. You go online to a joint venture site and meet someone in Africa who has access to hand woven purses from a village in the area. These purses are sold to tourists but no where else. The women in the village who make the purses do so to make a few extra dollars for their families. They can use the money and are selling the purses at a nominal amount of money.

Through your joint venture, you and your African business partner can sell the purses in the United States. Not only can you sell them in your store, you can also both agree to market your joint venture in a way that you can sell them online as well. Your customers in your shop are happy because they are getting unique purses that no one else has. You are happy because you are making more sales. Your African joint venture partner is happy because he is making money simply by buying the purses off of the village women and shipping them to you. And the women in the little village in Africa? Who would have thought that their handicrafts would be so coveted throughout the world. They are very happy as well. As you can see, there are many opportunities to be had when you enter into a joint venture with a foreign entity.

The negative aspects of being in a joint venture with a foreign entity include:

- No legal control over the other person
- Possibilities of miscommunication

While people like to think that they are legally protected if they enter into a joint venture with someone in the United States and have everything neatly signed and sealed, the reality is that lawyers cost money. A lot of money. You may have more legal control over someone in the United States, but are you going to spend the money to exercise that control?

If you have to take someone to court in the United States, it better be for more than $5,000. Less than that and you will have a difficult time getting a lawyer to represent you as this is considered to be small claims. If you have a sizable lawsuit, you may be able to get a lawyer to represent you, but they are going to want some money up front. Although you may have legal rights and can win a lawsuit if you go to court, the cost of going to court is often more than the suit is worth. Chances are even if the person is in the same town as you and wrongs you, you will not get your lost money.

You are better off to enter into any joint venture with a little bit of capital. Only when the trust between you and your joint venture partner has increased with time should you increase your investment, and still - only if he or she does the same.

Starting a joint venture with a foreign entity does have some risks, but it might be well worth it if you can find someone who you can trust. You may both end up reaping the rewards of such a joint venture.

Chapter 9 - Marketing Your Joint Venture

One way to maintain a good joint venture is to make sure that you market your joint venture. You and your joint venture partner should both be willing to share in the marketing of your business that you now have together.

You can use a variety of different marketing tools to get the word out about your business. Remember that the more people know about your business, the better off for both of you.

In some cases, you may find that your marketing partner has more expertise in the field of marketing than you. Or he or she may be more computer proficient. Everyone has some type of gift, so see which of your gifts you can bring to the table.

Ways that you can market your joint venture include the following:

- A website
- Direct marketing
- Indirect marketing

You should use all of the above when you are trying to market your joint venture online as all are effective forms of advertising.

Website

One of the first things that you will want to start is your own website. Your new business should have a website as a base. Whatever it is you are selling should be placed on this website. Not only is the website a way to market your new joint venture, but it will also be a way to showcase your existing business and that of your partner.

You should come up with a name that you will both like for your joint venture and then try to think of a good domain name. You are better off to get a domain name that is easy to remember, spell and will come up in the search engines. You and your joint venture partner should split the cost of registering the domain name and hosting the website.

If your joint venture partner knows how to start a website and can create one for the business, you should kick something in like pay for the domain name registration and a few months of hosting. This way, no one will feel like they have been taken advantage of and your partner can build a good site. You should both communicate with one another as to how you want the site to look and what you expect it to do for your business. Both of you should have access to the site at all times.

Most businesses today are either trying to start websites or already have websites. As we become more accustomed to using the internet in our daily lives, business owners are realizing how important it is to have a business website. It is similar to having a telephone in today's world. A website is a good way to let people know who you are and what you do.

Direct Marketing

Direct marketing is the most expensive way to get the word out about your business, but is the most effective. This involves contact from your business directly to your customers. You normally would use an internet service to provide you with direct marketing as it can be more time consuming than it would be worth to try to do this yourself.

Most direct marketing is sent to potential customers as well as existing customers. You should have demographics as to who your target market is and those are the individuals who will be getting your direct marketing advertising.

Direct marketing for your joint venture can consist of newsletters, press releases, e-mail ads and even coupons that are designed to introduce your business to the customer. Some direct marketing will ask for a response. A coupon is a form of direct response marketing as it requires the target to act right away.

You can find several sites online that will offer you direct marketing for your business at nominal rates. If you have a knack for writing, you can offer to write the newsletters and other ads for your business and perhaps your joint venture partner will kick in more money towards the direct marketing fees. Or vice versa.

Indirect Marketing

Indirect marketing is not as effective as direct marketing but is usually free. Some examples of how you can use indirect marketing to advertise your joint venture include:

- Writing articles for Ezine sites

- Posting links and information in forums
- Using social networking sites to talk about your business
- Using chatrooms
- Giving away free products

One of the most effective ways that you can use to market your business for free on the internet is to write an article for a free site and post it. The article should be written as a news style article. You should use your domain name as your user name on the site where you write these articles. Two places online where you can post articles that will be printed for all to see and where you can choose any user name are Ezine Articles and Associated Content. You can retain rights to the articles, post them online and draw people to your business website.

When you write an article that will be put on the internet, you should make sure that you use keywords that relate to your business. Keywords should be placed strategically throughout the article so that it is picked up in the search engines. The more people who read your article, the more exposure for your joint venture.

Another way to indirectly market your joint venture is to post links to your website in forums. You should use this sparingly as you will soon be seen as being "forum spamming." Although this is an effective form of marketing, you might end up getting kicked off the forums.

Social networking sites are another way to reach the masses. You can subtly use these sites to chat with others about what you are doing in your business and introduce others to your business. You can do the same when you are marketing in chatrooms.

Because the internet allows us all to be anonymous, you do not have to state that you are the owner of the business when you are in a chatroom or forum - you can simply guide others to the business that helped you out.

You and your joint venture partner should both be in synch when it comes to marketing your joint venture. One of the best aspects of the joint venture is that you no longer have to rely solely upon your own ideas as you have someone else with whom you can share your thoughts. Both of your can bounce your marketing ideas off one another. Not only will this help you with your joint venture, but it will also teach you a thing or two of how to improve the marketing for any other business endeavor that you might have.

Chapter 10 - Starting Your Joint Venture

Once you are ready to start your joint venture, you may wish to draw up a contract between you and your partner so that you both understand the obligations of the agreement. Even if the agreement is not legally binding, it is still a good idea to draw up something in writing. This gives you both an opportunity to say what you expect from the partnership and what you will be willing to give.

If you are starting a joint venture with someone who you met on the internet, you can use the internet to draw up the agreement and e-mail it to one another. If you want to have something in writing that will be binding, you can use a courier service to send the contracts back and forth so that you can both read, understand and sign them. Contracts should be signed in duplicate, or in the amount of however many joint venture partners that there are.

If you are starting a joint venture with someone in the United States, you may choose to open a checking account. One way that you can both be protected is to open an account that need two signatures for withdrawal. This way, neither person can take the money without the signature of the other party. The account should be held in the name of the joint venture. If you are holding the account as individuals and are not using joint venture name, it should be held not as joint tenants but as tenants in common.

Starting a joint venture with someone online can be exciting. Thanks to modern technology, you can not only formulate your agreement online, but you can communicate online as well. You can set up a chat room where the two of you can chat with one another about the business on a daily basis.

If you are using an attorney to draw up the agreement, you should pick someone who is used to preparing such agreements and is agreeable to both of you. If you are not using an attorney, or if you are entering into a joint venture with a party from another country, you may want to use some of the online forms for entering into a joint venture. This will enable you to enter into the agreement without having to pay an attorney.

If you decide to incorporate your joint venture business, or if you are creating an LLC or a limited partnership, you can find online vendors who will be glad to do this for you. You can pay a small fee plus the filing fee to incorporate your business.

Those who are entering into an agreement with someone from another country can open an offshore account where both of you have control over the funds. Take a look at the different avenues that are open to you with regard to offshore accounts. You will find that there are many places where you can open an account that will protect both of you.

You may want to invest in a system like Skype where you can make international calls through your computer without it costing you any money if you are doing a lot of business with people in other countries. This is a lot cheaper than trying to call someone from a land phone if they are overseas.

Starting your joint venture with your new partner will be exciting for both of you. You will want to continue to make it grow so that it becomes a profitable venture. Whether it is a small joint venture or a large venture with large, corporate principals, a joint venture gives you the option of being able to maximize the use of your business and capital without incurring all of the risk.

Chapter 11 - 10 Reasons To Start A Joint Venture

Why start a joint venture? There are plenty of reasons. Here are 10 good reasons why you should consider starting a joint venture:

1. It gives you access to more cash, more opportunity. You are not limited to your own capital, but you can use capital from your joint venture partner to enable not only your new business to flourish, but also your existing business. If you choose a good joint venture partner, the two of you are essentially doubling the value of your business.

2. It enables you to reach a new market. This is especially true when you enter into a joint venture with someone from another country. You have a whole new market in which to sell your product and so does your partner. Even if you just concentrate on selling each other's wares, you are helping each other make money.

3. You gain new knowledge. You can always learn something about your business, even if you have been operating a business for years. In exchange, you can also share your knowledge with another individual. Both of you will benefit from the joint venture.

4. You incur less risk. You can expand your business without incurring a lot of financial risk when you start a joint venture. Each party in the joint venture assumes some of the risk, which means that the risk is spread out evenly and no one stands to lose too much.

5. You can gain new marketing ideas. With both of you willing to market your new joint venture, you will most likely learn a thing or two from one another. By entering into a joint venture with someone else who is also creative and has good marketing ideas, you can both feed off of one another.

6. You can each use your own talents. Entering a joint venture can allow people who have a certain talent find someone who may need that talent to enable them to allow their business to grow.

7. You can invest using your knowledge. In some cases, you may be able to make an investment in something like a foreclosure or short sale with little or none of your own money. If you get enough partners in your joint venture who are willing to put up some of the money for the venture, you may be able to use your expertise to make money for them as well as yourself.

8. You have double the capital. Depending on how many people you recruit into your joint venture, you can have double or even triple the capital that you would have if you were starting out a business on your own. This gives you a chance to start a business the right way.

9. It is a good way to get started working with partners. If you are looking for a long term business arrangement, it is a good idea to start out with a joint venture. This is not forever and can be a good way to see if you like working with business partners. Those who you enjoy working with may invite you or you may invite them to other projects.

10. It gets your business name out there. If you are looking to make a name for your business, this is the way to do it. The more people who know about your business, the better off for you. By starting a joint venture, you are allowing your business to get maximum exposure.

Chapter 12 - What Can Go Wrong In A Joint Venture

Just as things can go wrong with a business, things can also go wrong with a joint venture. Some of the things that can go wrong with a joint venture include the following:

Lack of communication between the principals. This is usually one of the most common problems of a joint venture. In order for the joint venture to work and continue to thrive, all parties must be able to communicate their needs. Lack of communication will kill any relationship - whether it is personal or business.

One dishonest person in the barrel. Another problem that can occur with a joint venture is if you get someone who is dishonest or otherwise unscrupulous in the joint venture. They may try cheating their partners or individuals. Neither is good. If you are associated with them, you will most likely be lumped into the same category as them. You may even be liable for damages. This is why it is so important to screen individuals with whom you are thinking of starting a joint venture and make sure that they have integrity.

One person dies or just stops working. This can happen as well. A person in the joint venture can die or may just give up the business with no explanation. This can be especially problematic when you are in business with someone from another country as it will be difficult to keep in touch with them. One way you can alleviate this problem is to each ask for references of three people who can vouch for the person and who you can contact if the person decides to stop working. Everyone should be willing to provide these references and they should be checked before the parties enter into the joint venture.

A coup occurs in the country where you have interests. If you decide to start a joint venture with an individual from another country, be aware of the political atmosphere in that country and if there is civil unrest. Although this does not happen in most countries, it does happen in others. Have a Plan B in case you see civil unrest in the country where you joint venture partner lives and keep track of the news in that country.

The joint venture partner is a fraud. For about $50, you can find out about your joint venture partner. There are various places online that will do a background check on your potential joint partner. You can each submit to such a check to make sure that each of you are who you say you are.

Something can always go wrong in any business that you undertake, even if it is your own. Being in business is a risk regardless of how you look at it. Understand the risks and start out small so that you are comfortable with the situation before allowing the venture to grow.

Chapter 13 - Keeping Your Joint Venture Going Strong

Now that you are prepared to start your joint venture, follow this advice to keep your joint venture running smoothly and going strong:

Communication

Communication is the key to any relationship - business or otherwise. Without good communication, your business will break down and so will your joint venture. If you feel that the other party is taking advantage of you or is not pulling his share, you may be tempted to wait it out and see if they straighten out - after all, no one likes confrontation.

You have to have open lines of communication in order for the joint venture to continue to thrive. A good way to do this is to schedule weekly or even daily meetings where you can go over progress of the joint venture, sales or anything else that is on your mind. Regular meetings help keep the communication lines open.

Access Talents

Everyone has different sets of talents. Make sure that both you and your partner take advantage of each others talents for your joint venture. By allowing your natural talents in. you will each be doing a service not only to the joint venture, but to your own businesses as well. This also allows parties to feel part of the business and gives everyone involved a boost of self confidence. Nothing is better than being asked to do something because you have a talent for this project.

Have a written agreement.

The purpose of a written agreement is not to try to legally bind someone to something but to put down, in writing, what you expect from the joint partnership and what you are willing to give. By making this clear on all sides, you will be giving your joint venture an opportunity to grow. When all parties know what their roles are in a business, it make it easier for everyone to carry out those roles and allows business to flow smoother.

A joint venture can be a very profitable endeavor for anyone. This can be true if the partner is a person who lives in the next town or halfway across the world. It enables you to grow both as a joint venture business and a human being. The more insight that you have into the way that other people do business, the easier it is to allow your business to flourish.

When you start out looking for a joint venture, you will most likely look for someone who has similar interests and talents as you. Try to look for someone whose talents will compliment yours and truly make your business grow. Your ideal joint venture partner may not be someone who is exactly like you, but someone who will be willing to work with you, using their talents while you use yours, to start a very profitable joint venture.

In time, the joint venture can become not just a business, but a steady friendship and a common interest as you both strive to make your joint venture one that continues to flourish, expand and be profitable.

www.ingramcontent.com/pod-product-compliance
Lightning Source LLC
Chambersburg PA
CBHW041617180526
45159CB00002BC/899